The Beginner's Guide to Amazon Advertising

Don't Waste Your Money on Poor PPC Learn the Insider Secrets and Dominate Amazon Advertising Today!

By Andy Gelder: 6 figure Amazon Seller, Author and Entrepreneur

Introduction

Hi there, my name is Andy Gelder. I am a UK based Amazon seller and I have been selling on Amazon since the summer of 2015 when I launched my first brand on Amazon.com selling Pet Supplements.

I have recently launched into the Home and Kitchen Category in the UK with a plan to extend the brand to other Amazon marketplaces.

Over the years I have spent a small fortune learning about, and refining Amazon PPC. I dread to think about the mistakes I have made along the way and how much they have cost me LOL. I'm going to share those HARD-WON secrets with you today in this book.

So, I have written this Amazon PPC Beginners Guide for 2 reasons

1 - I want to try and help save you your money (it's better in your pocket than in Jeff Bezos' right!)

2 - It is so important to understand how the ads work and how they can skyrocket your sales. I want you to know how to set your Campaigns up correctly from the get-go. As a new seller, it's soooooo important to get this right otherwise you could literally burn through thousands of dollars, pounds, euros, or whatever currency you are using.

Are you ready? Let's get going

Chapter 1 What is Amazon PPC?

In a nutshell, Amazon PPC is a tool offered by Amazon to Sellers on Amazon to advertise their products which are for sale on Amazon - simples eh!

If you are an Amazon shopper (who isn't LOL) then you may or may not have noticed when you are searching for your product that sometimes you see the words "SPONSORED" underneath a particular product? The seller of this product has paid Amazon to get it in front of your eyes (he or she will pay if you click on the advert) - This is a Sponsored Product with a "Pay Per Click" Campaign behind it. There are 3 main types of Advertising Campaigns, I have listed them below so you understand them BUT as this is a Beginner's Book, I am focusing on "Sponsored Products" as the other 2 may not be available to you just yet

Sponsored Products - these enable you, the Seller to promote your individual product on the Amazon pages, in Search results and on Product Detail Pages. These are the most common types of adverts and the easiest to set up. They are available to all sellers.

Jellycat Bashfuls Medium Calf

⭐⭐⭐⭐⭐ ⌄ 541

£33⁷⁵

Get it **Thursday, Mar 4**
FREE Delivery by Amazon
Only 8 left in stock

15,799 in Toys & Games (Top 100)
883 in Soft Toys

ASIN: B001D7ETX8   `4 FBA Sellers`

`Price History` `Keepa History`

Little Jellycat - Bashful Bunny Cream - Baby Comfort Blanket

⭐⭐⭐⭐½ ⌄ 33

£23⁰⁰

Get it **Thursday, Mar 4**
FREE Delivery by Amazon
Only 4 left in stock

Ages: 0 months and up

12,004 in Baby Products (Top 100)
292 in Nursery Blankets

ASIN: B005J3PPW6   `8 FBA Sellers`

Jellycat Ballerina Unicorn Plush Toy (DD6U)

⭐⭐⭐⭐⭐ ⌄ 71

£54⁹⁹

Get it **Thursday, Mar 4**
FREE Delivery by Amazon
Only 8 left in stock

Ages: 1 month and up

174,711 in Toys & Games (Top 100)
11,672 in Soft Toys

ASIN: B0796NPZZY   `1 FBA Seller`

Jelly
Bun

⭐⭐

£26

Get i
FREE
Only

4⁵
2,

AS

Sponsored Brands - these type of adverts are for sellers who have a portfolio of products and are building a Brand (think Nike or Nescafe or Fitbit). These ads allow a seller to promote their brand with its logo plus a selection of products on a store page or a custom landing page.

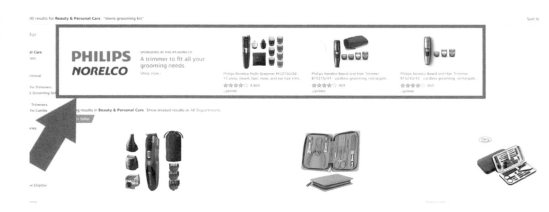

Sponsored Display Ads - these are ads that send the shopper to an Amazon Product Detail page (a mini website inside the main Amazon site) - it can target shoppers both on and off Amazon

The big advantage of Amazon PPC is that it is uniquely targeting shoppers on the Amazon platform. These shoppers are proven to have the intent to buy. Other advertising strategies will have to target shoppers in many different shopping journeys, but your Amazon PPC ads will target those shoppers who are loyal to Amazon and ready to buy - it makes your job and the job of your advert much easier.

Chapter 2 - Amazon PPC - Why do we need it?

As we all know, the Amazon platform has grown massively over recent years due to an organic growth in Online shopping plus the impact of Covid. The volume of shoppers has increased but what you may not realise is that the volume of sellers has also increased. This is in part due to an almost perfect storm - a proliferation of courses selling the "Amazon dream" and, because of covid, many people looking for alternative sources of income. Therefore, for your offering to stand out from the growing crowd it's essential that you consider a well set up and targeted ad campaign. There are literally millions of products and you do not want to get lost in all the noise, do you?

There is a joke in our Industry which goes something like this.

Q - "Where can you bury a body?
A - "Page 4 of Amazon"

The joke being that if your Product is not on Page 1 - 3 of Amazon then ...it, like the body in the joke, is buried. Geddit ?? I'll get my coat ahem.

Running a well-targeted Ad Campaign will also help you if there are important keywords on your Listing that are simply too competitive to rank for organically. Therefore, running a PPC campaign for those keywords will help gain Page 1 visibility and therefore drive more sales associated with that keyword which will help drive your product up the ranking for those keywords. It's a real sweet vicious circle!

There is also a particularly good case for you to run PPC campaigns on your own Products and best Keywords to "protect" them from a competitor. You are effectively "shutting the door" on the competition.

In conclusion, a correctly set up and managed Amazon PPC campaign will help you sell more products faster. It will also help increase your organic rankings therefore help you sell more products faster!

Chapter 3 - Basic Terms in use

It may seem a bit strange to have a "glossary" this early in a book, but I understand that many of my readers will be new to the subject. I want everything to be as clear as possible from the outset and for you to be able to follow my instructions in a logical, headache free way! Therefore, this next chapter includes some of the main "Basic Terms" - I have also included a fuller glossary at the end of the book.

Search Terms: These are the exact terms that a potential buyer types in the Amazon's search box at the top of the Amazon page. The results will be in order of all the advertisers bidding on those keywords and then the organic listings. It might be out of order, have other words attached to it, misspelled, or it may be an exact match.

Keywords: Amazon Keywords allow sellers to choose which search terms they want their ads to show up on Amazon. If a seller's Keyword matches the buyer's search term, then the ad will be shown to the buyer on Amazon.

Clicks: The number of times your ads were clicked on by a shopper (and therefore when you are charged). A click does not necessarily lead to a sale, but you will still be charged for it.

Conversion Rate: How well those "Clicks" convert into sales. 10 - 15% would be good. In simple terms, a shopper will click on an advert, if it's 100% relevant to their needs leading to 100% conversion rate

Impressions: The number of times your ads were displayed. Put another way - how many "eyes" were on your advert. It's important to also know how well Impressions convert to clicks - this is another measure of advert relevancy and is called "Click through Rate"

Cost Per Click: Simply how much each click costs and is abbreviated to CPC.

Advertising Cost of Sales (ACoS): In PPC terms this metric reveals what percentage of PPC sales is spent on advertising. You can calculate this by dividing total ad spend by PPC sales. For example, if you spent £40 on advertising , resulting in attributed sales of £400, your ACoS would be 10% (ie. £40 /£400 = 0.10 x 100).

To calculate your ideal maximum Advertising ACOS we need to work out the PROFIT as a percentage of the Selling price.
Let me use one of my products as an example for you.

Selling Price £33
Cost of Goods £4
All Amazon FBA fees £12
Misc (shipping from China plus prep and shipping to Amazon) £2.50

So, I subtract COG, Amazon fees and the Misc fees from the Selling price to leave me with a profit of £14.50.

To calculate my ACOS, I divide the profit by the Selling Price (14.50 / 33 = 0.43 x 100) = an ACOS of 43%

Meaning I have a nice healthy 43% margin that I COULD spend on advertising before I would be making a loss on my product from PPC costs.

Match types - this helps you to refine your targeting of the advert. There are 3 types of Match Types as follows:

Broad Match - it contains all your words in any order. Broad Match is often used as a further tool to research for additional, more relevant keywords.

Phrase Match - contains all your words in the same order individually or together.

Exact Match - contains ONLY your keywords and in the exact order.

These are some of the basic terms which are in common use, both on the Amazon PPC platform and in the world of Amazon advertising. They may seem totally confusing right now but as you start to run your own ads they will become much clearer and help you to understand the vast amount of data that Amazon has available to you.

I don't want to overwhelm you at this point, so have deliberately kept this chapter as simple as possible, focusing on the terminology that you are most likely to encounter as you begin your PPC journey.

Chapter 4 Setting up your first campaign.

Ok - so now I have covered some of the basics, let's get you set up and running with your first campaigns.

As we are approaching this book with the beginner in mind, the most effective way to start in Amazon advertising is as follows.

1 - set up an "Automatic Campaign" on JUST ONE product - then validate, optimise, and assess the Campaign

2 - Later, set up Manual Campaigns - optimise, assess and test

There are several reasons I am a fan of this strategy.

Firstly - an "Auto" Campaign takes a lot of the legwork out of the process. In simple terms you set the campaign up with some basic numbers on one product and you let it run on Autopilot for a predetermined time period. You then go back to the Campaign, analyse the data, and make decisions based on that data. It's a nice simple clean process that, for a beginner, is a good introduction to the PPC platform. If you follow my plan, then the risk of this campaign costing a lot of money will be reduced or indeed removed as you will have full control.

Let's get stuck into creating our very first "Automatic Campaign".

1 - Log in to your Seller Central Account then select "Advertising / Campaign Manager

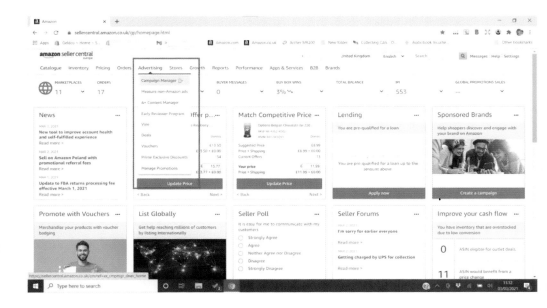

2 - Then, scroll down the page until you see the Yellow "Create Campaign" button - click this.

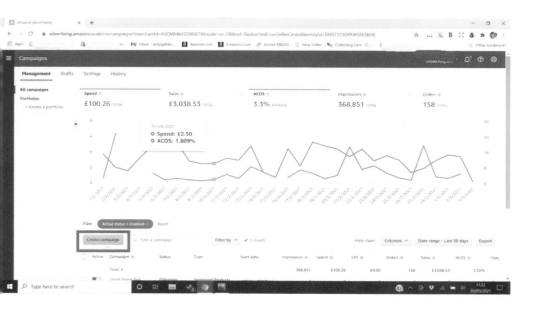

Ignore the chart on my screenshot with those blue and orange lines - this is an existing campaign and not relevant to our demonstration today.

3 - Then from the next 3 options choose "Sponsored Products."

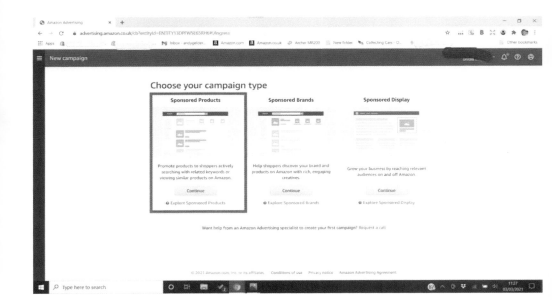

4 - Next page we need to start inputting some data and choose the name of our Campaign

Campaign Name - When choosing "Campaign names", it's really important to create a "Naming System" that is consistent, simple, will grow and flow through all your Products plus identify the type of Campaign - start with a system now as best practice.

Eg - "Auto Garlic Press"

Input your chosen name in the "Campaign Name" field.

Start Date / End Date - you can adjust either of these to suit yourself. You can advance the start date if you wish the Campaign to start work at some date in the future. If you want your Campaign to run "indefinitely" then simply leave the "END" date blank - I recommend doing this so long as you remember that the Campaign is running. I will come to other reasons later in the book.

Daily Budget - set this to the maximum you want to spend IN TOTAL for the duration of the Campaign divided by the daily duration of the Campaign - e.g., if you are going to initially run this for 10 days and your budget is £250 then the daily budget is £25.

However - most of your ads will likely cost between 0.75p - £1.75 - possibly a lot more if you are in an expensive niche like Supplements or Pets. Therefore, a low

Daily Budget of say £10 will quickly get used up. I would suggest a Daily Budget of approx. £25 initially.

The Daily Budget is a "guide amount" sometimes Amazon will spend it all, sometimes not. Some days they will spend MORE than the Daily Budget you have set but they will average it out over 7 days.

Scrolling further down the page you have the option to select the "Targeting" Type. There are three types of campaign-bidding strategies for automatic-targeting sponsored product ads.

Ensure that the "Automatic Targeting" radio button is ACTIVE and selected.

Dynamic bids – down only
Amazon lowers bids in real time when you are less likely to make a sale. This prevents your ad from showing up on irrelevant product searches.

Dynamic bids – up and down
In addition to lowering your bid as a 'down only' bid would, Amazon will increase the price of your bid by 10% if your automatic-targeting sponsored product is more likely to convert,

Fixed bids
You set your bid and Amazon does not change it – unless you choose to adjust it.

My Suggestion is to select "Dynamic Bids Up & Down. This will maximize your opportunities to gain sales.

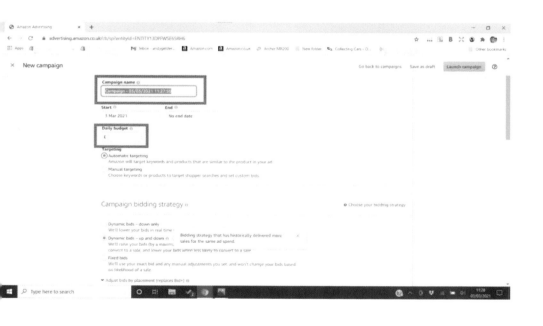

5- Creating an Ad Group and Selecting the Products

Naming the Ad Group

The ad group name should represent the Product (s) sharing the same bids and budgets - as I mentioned before, it can be anything, but I recommend naming the Group after the Campaign type (Manual or Auto) and the specific product.

Selecting Product to Advertise

If you are a new seller then it's likely that you will only have 1 product to select. In any case select the product you want to advertise by clicking the "ADD" button.

If you do have multiple products then simply scroll through the list OR input the ASIN and search for it.

6 - Setting the Default Bid.

This is where you set the price that you are prepared to pay (or BID) for the keywords. There are no set guidelines for this simply because a highly competitive keyword for a highly competitive product will cost you a lot more (I sell Pet Supplements and have seen Bids of $11 + !!) However, less competitive niches with fewer competitive Keywords will cost less. It's very much of "learning by experience" here and testing to see what you can find.

Amazon suggests starting at 0.75p, BUT I recommend starting your bid a little higher, possibly around £1.75 to £2.25 region to test the Campaign and discover more keywords. You can always reduce the bid later. There are also deeper more skilled strategies around Keyword mining which we will get into another time.

You will notice another Radio Button which allows you to select "Set Bids by Target Group" - this is a relatively new, more advanced feature which I do not recommend selecting at this point. It will likely overwhelm you with data and choices - we simply want to get a cost-effective ad campaign up and running.

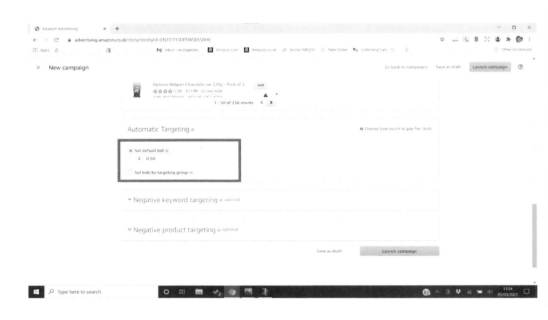

Then click the yellow "Launch Campaign" Button which takes you to the final page.

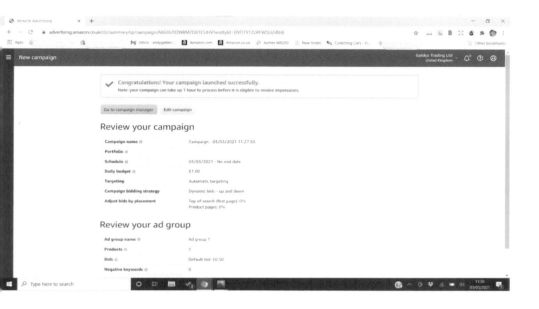

Your ad will shortly appear in your Campaign Manager. It usually takes around 20 minutes for it to appear on your Dashboard so do not panic if you don't see it right away.

Remember that you can always go back in to make any changes or edits. You can even delete it and start over again - it's not set in stone so do not be too concerned about making mistakes.

CONGRATULATIONS! Your FIRST Automatic Amazon Advert is now live!!

CHAPTER 5 - Monitoring and Optimizing your first Campaign.

With your first Auto Campaign it's good practice to let it run for 7 - 10 days before making any changes. Why do we do this?

The campaign needs a little time to get up and running to "bed-in" and to allow the advertising algorithm to start doing its work. That's why we leave it for at least the first 7 - 10 days.

I wouldn't leave it longer than 10 days without any analysis though - this is to prevent any costly, unprofitable Keywords or settings eating up your cash!

Your next steps are as follows (and don't worry, I'll walk you through the process in easy-to-manage steps shortly)

1 - Download and analyse the Search Term Report
2 - Find and Identify good keywords (keyword mining)
3 - Identify and remove expensive, non-relevant keywords (Optimising the Campaign)

So, let's get going, by jumping on to Step 1 - Download and analyse the Search Term Report

Go into your Seller Central Back Office and select Reports / Advertising Reports. This takes you to the "Reports" section of Amazon Advertising. It does look a little different to the regular Seller Central pages that you might be used to seeing - but do not worry, you are in the right place

Then click the Yellow "Create Report" button.

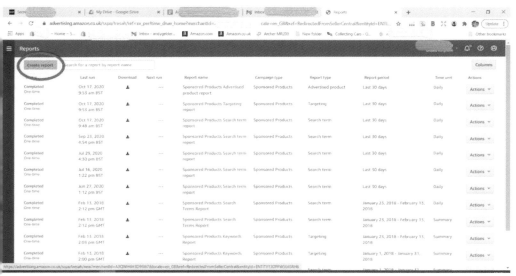

Assuming that you are a Beginner then you will not have the list of reports that I have on the screenshot above so do not worry if your screen looks different to mine - the good news is that every time you generate a report, Amazon saves it for a period of time for you – that's the list below.

Your next steps

Once that's done refresh the page and "Download" the report

It will download to your PC as an Excel Document so click and open it.
You may need to "Enable Editing" in Excel to allow you to make the next changes.

At this point I like to set up the Spreadsheet to allow you to search in the spreadsheet and filter it.

Firstly, click on the #1 in the top left corner. This will highlight the entire top row then, Sort and Filter / Filter. This adds little "filter" drop downs to each column which will help us in future.

Our first step is to identify keywords with 3 + sales and a good ACOS (refer to the ACOS section earlier to determine your ACOS) - we will mark these as GREEN and we are going to keep these for our EXACT campaign which we will set up next.

Our second step is to identify keywords with 1 or 2 sales and a good ACOS - we will mark these in ORANGE and keep them for our Broad and Phrase Campaigns which we will set up in the next step.

In my example below, my product has an ACOS of 32% so I am simply looking down the ACOS column for anything UNDER 32 % with 1, 2, 3 or more sales and colouring the rows appropriately. To make this job easier, I have sorted the ACOS column by clicking on the little arrow and "sort largest to smallest."

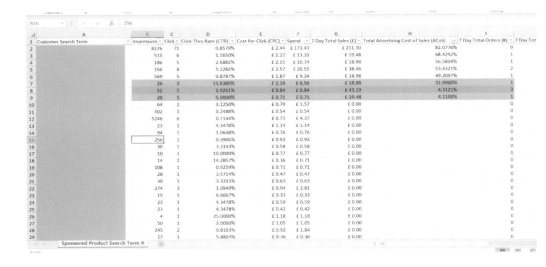

	A	B	C	D	E	F	G	H	I	
1	Customer Search Term	Impression	Click	Click-Thru Rate (CTR)	Cost Per Click (CPC)	Spend	7 Day Total Sales (£)	Total Advertising Cost of Sales (ACoS)	7 Day Total Orders (#)	7 Day Tot
2		8276	71	0.8579%	£ 2.44	£ 173.43	£ 211.30	82.0776%	9	
3		515	6	1.1650%	£ 2.22	£ 13.33	£ 19.48	68.4292%	1	
4		186	5	2.6882%	£ 2.15	£ 10.74	£ 18.98	56.5859%	1	
5		156	8	5.1282%	£ 2.57	£ 20.55	£ 38.46	53.4321%	2	
6		569	5	0.8787%	£ 1.87	£ 9.34	£ 18.98	49.2097%	1	
7		26	3	11.5385%	£ 2.19	£ 6.56	£ 18.98	31.9900%	1	
8		52	1	1.9231%	£ 0.84	£ 0.84	£ 43.19	4.3121%	3	
9		20	1	5.0000%	£ 0.71	£ 0.71	£ 19.48	4.1100%	1	
10		64	2	3.1250%	£ 0.79	£ 1.57	£ 0.00		0	
11		402	1	0.2488%	£ 0.54	£ 0.54	£ 0.00		0	
12		5246	6	0.1144%	£ 0.73	£ 4.37	£ 0.00		0	
13		23	1	4.3478%	£ 1.14	£ 1.14	£ 0.00		0	
14		94	1	1.0638%	£ 0.76	£ 0.76	£ 0.00		0	
15		256	1	0.3906%	£ 0.93	£ 0.93	£ 0.00		0	
16		30	1	3.3333%	£ 0.58	£ 0.58	£ 0.00		0	
17		10	1	10.0000%	£ 0.77	£ 0.77	£ 0.00		0	
18		14	2	14.2857%	£ 0.36	£ 0.71	£ 0.00		0	
19		108	1	0.9259%	£ 0.71	£ 0.71	£ 0.00		0	
20		28	1	3.5714%	£ 0.47	£ 0.47	£ 0.00		0	
21		30	1	3.3333%	£ 0.63	£ 0.63	£ 0.00		0	
22		274	3	1.0949%	£ 0.94	£ 2.81	£ 0.00		0	
23		15	1	6.6667%	£ 0.33	£ 0.33	£ 0.00		0	
24		23	1	4.3478%	£ 0.59	£ 0.59	£ 0.00		0	
25		23	1	4.3478%	£ 0.42	£ 0.42	£ 0.00		0	
26		4	1	25.0000%	£ 1.18	£ 1.18	£ 0.00		0	
27		50	1	2.0000%	£ 1.05	£ 1.05	£ 0.00		0	
28		245	2	0.8163%	£ 0.92	£ 1.84	£ 0.00		0	
29		17	1	5.8824%	£ 0.36	£ 0.36	£ 0.00		0	

Sponsored Product Search Term R

You will see at Lines 7 and 9, there are two keywords in the Customer Search Term column that are Orange and one at Line 8 that is green. What's happened here?? Well, you have successfully mined three good keywords for later use.

Next up we are going to identify and eliminate the costly keywords - this is the first step in a process of "optimisation."

I want you to organise and filter your "Spend" column (in my example, it's column F). Do it from "Largest to Smallest", by using the little arrow on the spreadsheet next to the word "Spend"?

You are going to look for Keywords with an ACOS that exceeds your target ACOS, that have 5 or more clicks AND 0 sales.

Also look for any Keywords that are not relevant to your product - for example, if you were selling Coloured Chalk Pens and you saw that a customer had searched "Coloured felt tip pens" - you need to stop that happening again.

You are going to mark these as RED and then "Negative Match" them in the Campaign. Negative Matching is an optimisation tool that Amazon gives us to allow us to prevent our adverts being shown to specific searches. There are two types - Negative Exact and Negative Phrase. We are going to use Negative Exact. I'll show you how to set it up.

	A	B	C	D	E	F	G	H	I	J	K
1	Customer Search Term	Impression	Click	Click-Thru Rate (CTR)	Cost Per Click (CPC)	Spend	7 Day Total Sales (£)	Total Advertising Cost of Sales (ACoS)	7 Day Total Orders (#)	7 Day Total Units (#)	7 Day Convers
2	glucosamine for dogs	4270	71	0.8570%	£ 2.44	£ 173.45	£ 211.30	82.0270%	9	11	
3	glucosamine and chondroitin for dogs	150	8	5.3267%	£ 2.57	£ 20.55	£ 30.46	53.4325%	3	3	
4	glucosamine for dogs	515	6	1.1650%	£ 2.22	£ 13.31	£ 35.44	44.4252%	1	1	
5	glucosamine dogs	190	5	2.6682%	£ 2.15	£ 10.74	£ 18.94	56.5859%	1	1	
6	dog joint supplements	2090	5	0.2392%	£ 1.65	£ 9.91	£ 0.00		1	1	
7	glucosamine and chondroitin dogs	509	5	0.8767%	£ 1.87	£ 9.36	£ 16.99	90.2097%	1	1	
8	glucosamine chondroitin for dogs	141	4	2.8369%	£ 2.11	£ 8.42	£ 0.00		0	0	
9	glucosamine for dog	234	4	1.7094%	£ 1.89	£ 7.54	£ 0.00		0	0	
10	dog supplements	199	3	1.5075%	£ 2.44	£ 7.32	£ 0.00		0	0	
11	hip and joint for dogs	26	3	11.5385%	£ 2.19	£ 6.56	£ 18.98	31.9900%	1	1	
12	joint supplement for dog	156	3	1.9231%	£ 1.92	£ 5.77	£ 0.00		0	0	
13	b003w5vdwo	5246	6	0.1144%	£ 0.73	£ 4.37	£ 0.00		0	0	
14	joint joint care supplements	174	2	1.1494%	£ 1.85	£ 3.69	£ 0.00		0	0	
15	glucosamine dog	34	2	5.8824%	£ 1.70	£ 3.40	£ 0.00		0	0	
16	joint supplements for dogs	171	2	1.1696%	£ 1.61	£ 3.21	£ 0.00		0	0	
17	joint and hip supplement for dogs	4	1	25.0000%	£ 2.93	£ 2.93	£ 0.00		0	0	
18	b0131lzts2	274	3	1.0949%	£ 0.94	£ 2.81	£ 0.00		0	0	
19	dog supplement	22	1	4.5455%	£ 2.71	£ 2.71	£ 0.00		0	0	
20	joint aid for dogs	94	1	1.0638%	£ 2.50	£ 2.50	£ 0.00		0	0	
21	dog joint supplement	23	1	4.3478%	£ 2.33	£ 2.33	£ 0.00		0	0	
22	joint aid dogs	43	1	2.3256%	£ 2.23	£ 2.23	£ 0.00		0	0	
23	joint supplement dogs	153	1	0.6536%	£ 2.06	£ 2.06	£ 0.00		0	0	
24	b01tnjs56	245	2	0.8163%	£ 0.92	£ 1.84	£ 0.00		0	0	
25	glucosamine supplements for dogs	1	1	100.0000%	£ 1.66	£ 1.66	£ 0.00		0	0	
26	b003u8l1nq	64	2	3.1250%	£ 0.79	£ 1.57	£ 0.00		0	0	
27	b077j3evcp	84	2	2.3810%	£ 0.78	£ 1.55	£ 0.00		0	0	
28	dog joint care	6	1	16.6667%	£ 1.45	£ 1.45	£ 0.00		0	0	
29	dog joint	50	1	2.0000%	£ 1.39	£ 1.39	£ 0.00		0	0	

Sponsored Product Search Term R

To add a "Negative Keyword" we simply go into the relevant Campaign, click "NEGATIVE KEYWORD" then Copy & Paste the Red Highlighted Keywords we identified, from earlier.

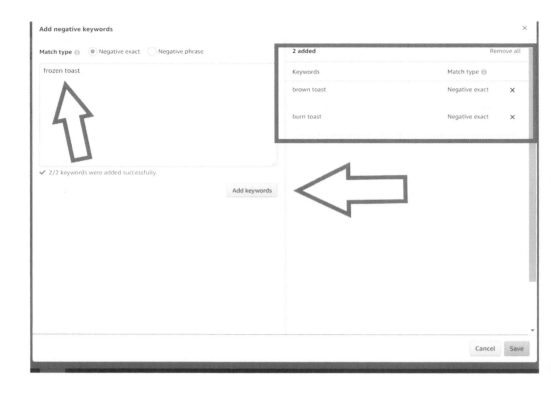

Frozen Toast is about to be added - remember to ensure the "NEGATIVE EXACT" Radio button is selected.

Brown Toast and Burnt Toast have already been added as Negative Exact matches

Click SAVE when finished and you are done!!!

Earlier, I mentioned that there are two types of Negative Matches. Negative Phrase is a less precise match type, and it would be used, for example, if you were selling a dog supplement and you noticed that you were getting a lot of Customer

Searches for HORSE supplements. If this type of match is not relevant to your product you may consider simply adding the word "Horse" as a Negative Phrase.

This way, your advert will not be displayed to anyone searching for HORSE.

What about all those pesky ASINs in your report?

You will likely notice that your Search Term report contains lots of other Sellers ASIN's. These appear because the Shopper has landed on your detail page after your advert was displayed on that corresponding ASIN's Listing Page.

At the time of writing, there is nothing we can do about this BUT the data is useful for future Advertising Campaigns because you can target those ASINs in different types of campaigns. For now, just accept it as an Amazon anomaly I'm afraid.

Customer Search Term	Impression	Click	Click-Thru Rate (CTR)	Cost Per Click (CPC)	Spend	7 Day Total Sales (£)	Total Advertising Cost of Sales (ACoS)	7 Day Total Orders (#)	7 Day Total Units (#)	7 Day Convers
	8276	71	0.8579%	£ 2.44	£ 173.41	£ 211.30	82.0776%	9	11	
	515	6	1.1650%	£ 2.22	£ 13.33	£ 19.48	68.4292%	1	1	
	186	5	2.6882%	£ 2.15	£ 10.74	£ 18.98	56.5859%	1	1	
	156	8	5.1282%	£ 2.57	£ 20.55	£ 38.46	53.4321%	2	2	
	569	5	0.8787%	£ 1.87	£ 9.34	£ 18.98	49.2097%	1	1	
	26	3	11.5385%	£ 2.19	£ 6.56	£ 18.98	34.5627%	1	1	
	52	1	1.9231%	£ 0.84	£ 0.84	£ 43.19	4.3121%	3	1	1
	20	1	5.0000%	£ 0.71	£ 0.71	£ 19.48	4.1100%	1	0	
	64	2	3.1250%	£ 0.79	£ 1.57	£ 0.00		0	0	
b003w5rrgu	402	1	0.2488%	£ 0.54	£ 0.54	£ 0.00		0	0	
b003w5vdwo	5246	6	0.1144%	£ 0.73	£ 4.37	£ 0.00		0	0	
b003ggahl8	23	1	4.3478%	£ 1.14	£ 1.14	£ 0.00		0	0	
b003zge5sy	94	1	1.0638%	£ 0.76	£ 0.76	£ 0.00		0	0	
b00a7mi7xs	256	1	0.3906%	£ 0.93	£ 0.93	£ 0.00		0	0	
b00gnl0y92	30	1	3.3333%	£ 0.58	£ 0.58	£ 0.00		0	0	
b00ilm0w8e	10	1	10.0000%	£ 0.77	£ 0.77	£ 0.00		0	0	
b00jf0shce	14	2	14.2857%	£ 0.36	£ 0.71	£ 0.00		0	0	
b00pcnblvy	108	1	0.9259%	£ 0.71	£ 0.71	£ 0.00		0	10	
b00um3j790	28	1	3.5714%	£ 0.47	£ 0.47	£ 0.00		0	0	
b00xib5q4s	30	1	3.3333%	£ 0.63	£ 0.63	£ 0.00		0	0	
b0131lzts2	274	3	1.0949%	£ 0.94	£ 2.81	£ 0.00		0	0	
b01ak476fw	15	1	6.6667%	£ 0.33	£ 0.33	£ 0.00		0	0	
b01bu2se6i	23	1	4.3478%	£ 0.59	£ 0.59	£ 0.00		0	0	
b01j97rvtk	23	1	4.3478%	£ 0.42	£ 0.42	£ 0.00		0	0	
b01ldhcwf4	4	1	25.0000%	£ 1.18	£ 1.18	£ 0.00		0	0	
b01lg8w4hq	50	1	2.0000%	£ 1.05	£ 1.05	£ 0.00		0	0	
b01lrnjs56	245	2	0.8163%	£ 0.92	£ 1.84	£ 0.00		0	0	
	17	1	5.8824%	£ 0.36	£ 0.36	£ 0.00		0	0	

Sponsored Product Search Term R

Chapter 6 - Creating your Manual Campaigns.

So, we have now done some basic keyword mining using the Auto Campaign and I'm now going to show you how to use these "mined" keywords that we know are relevant to your product and add them into a Manual Campaign.

I will also show you how to use some freely available tools to discover other keywords to test.

Before we start it's worth explaining the difference between the three different match types used on Amazon. They are BROAD, PHRASE and EXACT.

Amazon explains it like this -

Broad match: This match type offers your ad broad traffic exposure. A search term will match if it contains all the keyword terms in any order. Broad match also includes the plural form of the keyword, related searches, and other variations that are close to the keyword.

Phrase match: The search term must contain the exact phrase or sequence of words. It is more restrictive than broad match and will generally result in more relevant placements for your ad. Phrase match also includes the plural form of the keyword.

Exact match: The search term must exactly match the keyword or sequence of words for the ad to show and will also match close variations of the exact term. Exact match is the most restrictive match type but can be more relevant to a search. Exact match also includes the plural form of the keyword.

Or in another way -

If your Keyword is Garlic Press then

In a BROAD MATCH it will trigger with Garlic & Press in the search term, on their own separately, or together with other words (e.g., Fresh Garlic or Trouser Press)

In a PHRASE MATCH it will trigger together with words either before or after (e.g., Red Garlic Press or Garlic Press Set)

In an EXACT MATCH it will only trigger with Garlic Press. However, note that it allows for plurals, singular and bad spelling (Garlik Press, garlic presses!)

These terms do take a little getting used to. However, as you start drilling down into your ads you will quickly get used to the terminology - I promise!!

So, let's now move on to creating your Manual Campaigns. Jump back to Chapter 4 in this book and follow the "Create Campaign" process again - Steps 1 - 3.

When you get to Step 3, you need to follow this UNTIL you reach the Automatic radio button - at this point select MANUAL Targeting.

You need to give this Ad Group a name and remember that I told you it's important to create, then STICK TO ,a naming regime throughout your advertising portfolio.

I highly recommend the following regime.

1 - Product name/ Automatic

2 - Product Name / Manual / BR

3 - Product name / Manual / PH

4 Product Name / Manual / EX

I like to group all my Manual Ad Groups under one Campaign, so it looks like this.

Campaign Name = Product Name / Manual (e.g., Pizza Cutter / Manual)

Then inside the Campaign I will have my three match types as follows.

Pizza Cutter / Manual / BR

Pizza Cutter / Manual / PH

Pizza Cutter / Manual / EX

This allows me to set a budget for the entire Campaign but also to allocate that budget to each Ad group inside the Campaign and giving me much more control for future sorting and optimising. You may choose to structure your Campaigns differently of course as there are many ways to do this!

It's always possible to go back and change these names later BUT I prefer to get it set up correctly from the start. The naming regime has no impact on your Amazon adverts performance, but it allows you to better sort and manage your adverts in the future. Things can get quite complicated if you have 10 - 15 products, all with different campaign structures and names.

Right - let's move on. Select the product again (as per Chapter 4) and now follow the process below. We are going to create a BROAD match AD Group inside a new Campaign called "Pizza Cutter / Manual". The Broad Match AD Group will be called "Pizza Cutter / Manual / BR."

Create an ad group

An ad group is a group of ads sharing the same set of keywords and products. Consider grouping products that fall within the same category and price point range. You can edit your campaign after launch to create additional ad groups in campaign manager.

Settings	⊘ Create an ad group

Ad group name ⓘ

Pizza Cutter Manual BR

Products ⓘ	⊘ Add the products you want to advertise

Search   **Enter list**   Upload   0 products

Enter ASINs separated by a comma, space or new line.   ⟵   Target ASIN goes here

Add

Add products

Scroll down the page and ensure that "Keyword Targeting" radio button is selected. Now, enter your Keywords. This is a BROAD Ad Group so ensure that you UNTICK the Phrase and Exact Match Types.

Remember all the way back in Chapter 4 when we highlighted those Green and Orange Keywords in the spreadsheet? Well, this is where they come in useful - go back and grab the Yellow Keywords from the Search Term Column (in the example, they are greyed out but in column A)

Paste the ORANGE ones into the box.

Amazon may recommend a "suggested bid price" for these keywords. My recommendation at this point would be to increase the bid upwards to gain more sales and data. However, if you are in an extremely competitive niche with expensive keywords then keep a close eye on this as you will burn through your budget very quickly.

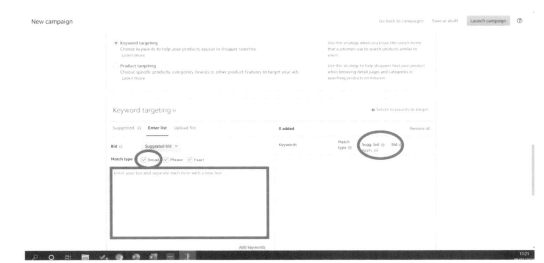

Almost done!

Just scroll down and hit "Launch Campaign."

Now you need to repeat the same process to create your Phrase Campaign, remembering to ensure the "Phrase" box is the only one ticked this time when you are creating the advert. Use the Orange keywords and add about 15% to the bid price when compared to the bid price you set in Broad. We do this to prevent the Keywords competing against each other.

Finally, repeat exactly again, this time creating your Exact advert making the changes to the names and ensuring the EXACT box is ticked. Input the Keywords from Customer Search Term Column A (in my example) that we coloured GREEN and again, add ANOTHER 15% to the Phrase bid you set earlier.

Do not forget to "Launch" your Campaigns ;-)

To tidy up your work now, I would grab all the green, yellow, and orange keywords and NEGATIVE EXACT MATCH them inside the auto campaign. I showed you how to do this earlier in the book so just grab the keywords and follow my steps, making sure that:

1 - you go into your correct Auto Campaign

2 - you click into "NEGATIVE KEYWORD"

3 – you add them as NEGATIVE EXACT

It's always possible to go in and remove or add to these in the future - in fact in my second, Advanced book I show you how to do this as it is a good practice to do so and forms part of your "optimisation regime."

So, you now have three Campaigns up and running. I would leave them for a further 7 - 10 days before taking action and the next steps will be.

1 - optimise these Campaigns and

2 - add more keywords

Sound familiar? Getting a touch of deja-vu?? I will come to both these processes in the next Chapters!

Adding additional keywords to your Campaign

At this point you are simply using keywords that you mined from your Automatic Campaign. This is an excellent first step. The keywords that you have "mined" from your own Auto Campaign will be highly relevant to YOUR product and should therefore get you some good value clicks and sales. However, you may only have added a few keywords from the Auto Campaign and ideally you need a good few more. How many more? Well, that is a "how long is a piece of string?" type question. From my experience, 6 - 10 keywords drive the majority of the sales BUT I would suggest you aim to compile a list of around 30 relevant keywords.

So how do you go about "harvesting" more keywords? Here are a few of my favourite sources and methods.

1 - Amazon Suggests. Did you that notice, that when you were inputting your "mined" keywords, there was a tab - Suggested Keywords? Amazon will "scrape" your product listing for appropriate keywords to use in the Campaign. Now - be aware that if your Listing is badly written with incorrect keywords then this will also pick them up. But "Amazon Suggests" is a great source of ideas. Make sure you add the correct "match type" into the correct AD GROUP – eg. add Phrase suggestions to your Phrase Advert.

2- AMZ Suggestion Expander is a free Chrome Extension that searches the Amazon Search facility when you type in a search. It then (rather cleverly) shows you other useful search ideas.

From the example below, I have typed "Pizza Cutter" in the search bar, and you will see the suggestions below from the App.

3 - If you have Jungle Scout or Helium 10 then you can use their free Keyword Scouting services - plus here are few more free and paid for tools that you can try - they all work on the same principle whereby you input your main Keyword (eg Pizza Cutter) and the tool will then return you a list of relevant, in depth (long - tail) keywords that you can test in your adverts.

Some of the more sophisticated tools will allow you to do a reverse search on a similar or competitor product but that's all for another day!!!

It's also exceptionally good practice to keep a Master List of your keywords on a text file or Excel document on your laptop.

Here are some of my favorite Software Tools

Helium 10, **Seller Tools** and **Jungle Scout** are comprehensive suites of tools for Amazon Sellers.

For Keyword analysis I suggest **Merchant Words, Keyword Tool and Keyword Inspector**.

Amazon's Seller Central can be confusing when you try to extract financial data for P&L etc so I HIGHLY recommend a Third Party piece of software. I have been helping the team at **Sumfully** with their beta tests and am SUPER IMPRESSED with its capabilities.

Chapter 8 - Optimising your Manual Campaigns.

I am assuming you followed my steps earlier in the book. You created and then optimised your first Auto Campaign? Good!! Because it will make your understanding of the next step so much easier. We are going to take what we learnt in Chapter 5 and apply the same principles to optimise your new Manual Campaigns.

Firstly, run an advertising report (exactly the same as the Chapter 4 process) Run through the Customer Search Terms for the Campaign that you are working on and check to ensure that you are not paying for any unrelated clicks - e.g., if you are selling a metal pizza cutter and paid for a click for Pizza Stone" for example, then you would want to Negative Exact "pizza stone".

Once you have checked for irrelevant keywords and clicks, it's time to fine-tune the keyword performance. It's now easy to do this on the Amazon platform itself. So, come back to the Campaign within Seller Central and click on the "Targeting" tab.

Then scroll down to the list of Keywords that you input in the previous step. Here, you can review the keyword performance and modify if needed. Note that you can modify the information displayed by clicking "Columns" then "Customise Columns" and editing as needed - Impressions, Clicks and ACOS are the basics that you need at this point, so adjust if needed.

	Active	Keyword	Match type	Status	Bid	Impressions	Clicks	CTR	Spend	CPC	Sales	▲ ACOS
		Total: 9				7,218	74	1.03%	£31.78	£0.43	£32.97	96.39%
☐	◉	led night li...	Phrase	Delivering	£ 0.58	945	4	0.42%	£1.58	£0.40	£10.99	14.56%
☐	◉	night light...	Phrase	Delivering	£ 0.77	4,816	44	0.91%	£21.95	£0.50	£21.98	99.86%
☐	◉	rainbow ni...	Phrase	Delivering	£ 0.50	1	1	100.00%	£0.48	£0.48	-	-
☐	◉	lights for gi...	Phrase	Delivering	£ 0.41	158	5	3.16%	£1.51	£0.30	-	-
☐	◉	rainbow ni...	Phrase	Delivering	£ 0.52	1	-	-	-	-	-	-
☐	◉	led bedroo...	Phrase	Delivering	£ 0.55	70	2	2.86%	£0.83	£0.42	-	-
☐	◉	baby night...	Phrase	Delivering	£ 0.58	597	7	1.17%	£2.49	£0.36	-	-
☐	◉	girls bedro...	Phrase	Delivering	£ 0.36	287	3	1.05%	£0.82	£0.27	-	-
☐	◉	rainbow light	Phrase	Delivering	£ 0.37	343	8	2.33%	£2.12	£0.27	-	-

Now - as per the Chapter about Optimising your Automatic Campaigns, I would suggest similar metrics when looking for keywords to optimise and as follows:

1 - look for Keywords with at least 10 clicks AND an ACOS that is greater than your threshold

If the ACOS is 100% greater then I would mark this keyword to be "Inactive" because it may well not be relevant to your product OR it's simply too competitive.

If the ACOS is only just above your threshold (e.g., 50%) then I would lower the bid - you simply click in the "Bid" field and input an increased number - I would likely double the bid at this point.

If there are 0 Impressions OR Clicks, then I would consider increasing the Bid, monitor for a further week and then see if the Impressions and Clicks start to increase.

2 - Remember to Negative Exact any poor performing or non - relevant keywords that you discover (either in the above step OR from the downloaded Search Term Report)

3 - Now add in any newly discovered keywords (following the same process that I discussed back in the Chapter about optimising your Automatic Campaign)

Keeping records of your changes - Amazon recently introduced a "History tab" which enables you to keep a track of changes you make to your Campaigns. For us old timers, this was a great revelation, BUT I am personally used to taking Before / After screenshots.

I like the visual comparisons - it is easier for me to visualise the changes I make and to monitor the results. So, I'm not a big user of the "History" tab BUT please feel free to explore either option. HOWEVER, know this - IT IS SUPER

IMPORTANT to monitor and test your Campaigns.

Amazon PPC advertising is like navigating a ship across the Ocean.
We know where we are going.
We kinda know how to get there.
But we need to make constant small adjustments along the way as winds and tides will knock us off course if we don't make those little tweaks and adjustments to our course.

Chapter 9 - In conclusion

I truly hope this book helps you, the beginner, to get started with your first Amazon PPC Campaign. My knowledge here is the results of 5 + years experimenting, testing and long hours pouring over spreadsheets!

You have probably realised that this is just "the tip of the iceberg" and that there is a whole world of methods, systems, and strategies to give you multiple ways to get more exposure and therefore sell more. There is plenty more to explore once you understand these basics! My goal here is to explode some of the myths surrounding Amazon PPC and to give you some of the basic building blocks which should serve you well. Please also be aware that Amazon is a constantly changing platform and that some of the principles or methods I have shown you MAY evolve, develop, or indeed completely vanish from the platform in time. However - get these basics RIGHT and you will have the tools to profitably grow your Business on Amazon. I sincerely wish you well.

You can contact me at : andy@andygelder.com

Glossary of Terms

- Keyword mining (or Harvesting) Use another source to discover relevant, new keywords.
- Impressions: The number of times your ads were displayed or viewed.
- Customer search term. This is the exact term that an Amazon customer used to find your product.
- Conversion rate. Your conversion rate is the number of sales made, divided by the number of impressions your sponsored product ad received in the same time frame.
- Clicks: The number of times your ads were clicked.
- Bid: The amount you are prepared to pay in an auction for your advert to be displayed
- Optimise: to refine and improve your adverts performance by tuning the keyword performance

Resources and References

The material in this book is drawn from my own Best Practices and the years I have spent selling on Amazon. I have made my best endeavours to check that the information is correct and current.

I would like to acknowledge the following resources. If I have inadvertently omitted to credit an author or source, then I apologize and invite you to contact me at andy@andygelder.com for inclusion in a future edition of this book or in a revision.

Nagaraj, A. (2018, April). *What is Amazon PPC. How An Amazon PPC Auction Works* SellerApp. https://www.sellerapp.com/blog/amazon-ppc-basics/

Saunders, M. (2021, January). *Amazon PPC: The Ultimate Guide (2021 Update).* sellics.com. https://sellics.com/blog-amazon-ppc-guide/

Dave Hamrick. (2021, January). *Amazon PPC Strategies* – The Ultimate Guide for 2021. Jungle Scout. https://www.junglescout.com/blog/amazon-ppc-best-practices/

Elias, M. (2020, August 15). *Amazon PPC Campaign Structure 101* https://www.helium10.com/blog/amazon-ppc-campaign-structure/

Advertising on Amazon. (2021, February 10).

https://sellercentral.amazon.co.uk/learn/courses?ref_=su_course_accordio

n&moduleId=526&courseId=147&modLanguage=English&videoPlayer=yo

utube

Printed in Great Britain
by Amazon